# KENNETH COPELAND

# THE
# POWER
## TO BE FOREVER
# FREE

**Harrison House**
Tulsa, Oklahoma

**The Power to Be Forever Free**

ISBN 1-57562-058-8

KC-058-8
30-0033

Published by Harrison House, Inc.
P. O. Box 35035
Tulsa, Oklahoma 74153

# The Power to Be Forever Free

"Disciplining the flesh." For many believers that phrase stirs memories of frustration and failure. They know it's important—the Word of God clearly teaches that. But they're not sure exactly how to go about it.

Some have given up, shrugging off such discipline as impossible. Others are still fighting stubbornly to get their flesh under control and losing one battle after another.

But it doesn't have to be that way. In fact, we can't afford to let it be that way. It will cost us too much! You and I are blessed to be part of the generation that will see the signs and wonders which the prophets of old wished they could have lived long enough to see. We will witness the Spirit of God poured out upon all flesh. But sin obstructs the Spirit's flow. And only as we rid ourselves of it will the power and glory of God be manifested through us. Only then will we experience the wonderful things that are prophesied to take place in our generation.

But is it really possible to step out of the sin you've struggled with so long—and live under the Spirit's control? Yes, it is! And the Word of God will show you how.

Hebrews 12:1-3 provides the key.

**Wherefore seeing we also are compassed about with so great a cloud of witnesses, let us lay aside every weight, and the sin which doth so easily beset us,**

**and let us run with patience the race that is set before us, Looking unto Jesus the author and finisher of our faith; who for the joy that was set before him endured the cross, despising the shame, and is set down at the right hand of the throne of God. For consider him that endured such contradiction of sinners against himself, lest ye be wearied and faint in your minds.**

Notice that this scripture doesn't just say to lay aside the weight and sin which so easily besets us. It says to look to Jesus. But how can you look to someone you can't see?

I did my best to look to the Lord the first five years I was born again, but I wanted to see Him with my natural eye. I thought that if I could just see Jesus in person, I could surely get rid of all the junk in my life. That would have been wonderful, but it didn't happen that way.

Then one day I saw Him in the Word. Oh, praise God! Now I know how to look to Jesus, the Author and Finisher of my faith, to help me to discipline myself. Actually, I discovered it quite by accident when Jesus delivered me from smoking.

When I was first born again, I was dominated by a horrible smoking habit. I tried to quit every way I could think of. I threw away so many full and nearly full packs of cigarettes while I was driving down the road, it seemed I threw away more than I smoked! But that didn't work. I'd just turn my car around and go back and get them.

My deliverance came as I was attending some meetings in Hilton Sutton's church in Houston, Texas. I had more respect for the preachers than to smoke in their presence, so I tucked my cigarettes in the sun visor in the car and left them there.

At that time I had been a Christian for quite a while, but I didn't know anything about the Word and had never been exposed to the power of God. When they started preaching under the anointing of the Holy Spirit, it held my attention. I was caught up in the living Word. My desires changed. All I wanted was more of God. For the first time in my life, the Scriptures came alive.

Brother Sutton preached on the second coming of Jesus, and I got really "high" on it. Suddenly I could hardly stand all the things that were wrong in my life. What happened? The Word replaced the desire to smoke. When those meetings ended and I started driving back home, I found those old, stale cigarettes tucked up in my sun visor and realized I hadn't even missed them!

I learned that the living Word of Almighty God is the only power that can cause me to think, look, talk and act like a born-again man. It's the only thing that can empower me to discipline this flesh of mine. When I saw Jesus in the Word, I was totally set free, not only of the habit, but of the desire!

It has not always been this way, though. I remember when the devil first entered my life. It seemed like such a small temptation to begin with, but it grew into a stronghold of the devil that nearly destroyed me. One afternoon as a 9-year-old boy, I just yielded to the temptation to "cuss." I knew better, but I did it anyway. I had a relative who was so good at West Texas "cussin'" that I thought he invented it! I was intrigued, and I wanted to try it.

When I let go of all restraint and began to say those cuss words, something evil moved in on my thinking that seriously affected me for some 20 years. Satan captured my mind that day and set a law in motion. My flesh gradually became boss over my entire being. By the age of 20, I was almost 100 pounds overweight and headed for destruction. A spiritual, scriptural illiterate, I was totally out of control and couldn't stop it.

I didn't know it at the time, but now I realize that Satan used a very subtle strategy—lasciviousness—to take control of my life. The word means "having no restraint."

Lasciviousness has been preached as being extreme immorality, but it doesn't start out that way. It begins with just a few seemingly innocent thoughts. Then those thoughts grow and grow until they begin to produce serious sin.

Lasciviousness comes wrapped in many different packages, but they all have the same result—destruction. The wages of sin is death. All sin is selfishness tied with a different bow. Sex sins, gluttony, etc., all stem from the "big me" and the result is the same. Satan only comes to steal, kill and destroy.

Ephesians 4:17-19 gives us some insight into the nature of lasciviousness. *"This I say therefore, and testify in the Lord, that ye henceforth walk not as other Gentiles walk, in the vanity of their mind, Having the understanding darkened, being alienated from the life of God through the ignorance that is in them, because of the blindness of their heart: Who being past feeling have given them-selves over unto lasciviousness, to work all uncleanness with greediness."*

Gentile in this context is a spiritual term meaning "without God." As Christians, born of His Spirit, we have His divine nature. Paul admonishes us to no longer live as though we were without God. We are to be controlled by our spirits which are recreated in His image and not be dominated by our carnal minds. You see, your natural mind is in enmity against God. But your spirit, if you are born again, is in harmony with Jesus. Satan uses lasciviousness to apply pressure to your flesh, so it will dominate your spirit and separate you from God.

Notice that Paul said, *"Who being past feeling...."* This means "to be dead to shame" or "to have the conscience seared until it is no longer effective." Satan's ultimate goal through lasciviousness is to cause you to live exactly like the rest of the world lives. Even though you may be born again and filled with the Spirit, he wants you to be guided by the vanity of your mind, separated from the nature of God which is in you.

The mind is the ground of Satan's seed. Second Corinthians 10:4-5 tells us how to keep his seed from taking root. *"(For the weapons of our warfare are not carnal, but mighty through God to the pulling down of strong holds;) Casting down imaginations, and every high thing that exalteth itself against the knowledge of God, and bringing into captivity every thought to the obedience of Christ."* Obedience to Christ and obedience to the Word are synonymous because Jesus is the Word.

If your mind is not renewed to God's Word, you will never be totally free of lasciviousness. It starts with having no restraint, first to thoughts which come innocently enough but result in throwing you totally out of control. For example, "Well, I know I shouldn't eat that, but just a little won't hurt." Oh really? You just swallowed the seed of your own destruction. You rationalized and thought, *Oh well, it's just a little.* But it never stops there. It grows until you find yourself exercising no restraint whatsoever.

The process is the same with every type of sin. Satan doesn't just blare out something like, *Why don't you kill someone today?* No! The devil is more subtle than that. He plants a tiny seed which grows into bigger and bigger things. Before he can drive someone to commit murder, he's got to get them to entertain thoughts of unforgiveness, resentment and revenge. They start out so small that you don't pay attention to them, but they grow.

Lasciviousness finally erodes the life of the born-again believer until he appears to be no different from an unregenerate man. The devil uses it to get you to think like the world thinks so that eventually you will act like the world acts. Carnal thoughts produce carnal actions. Jesus said:

**O generation of vipers, how can ye, being evil, speak good things? for out of the abundance of the heart the mouth speaketh. A good man out of the good treasure of the heart bringeth forth good things: and an evil man out of the evil treasure bringeth forth evil things. But I say unto you, That every idle word that men shall**

**speak, they shall give account thereof in the day of judgment. For by thy words thou shalt be justified, and by thy words thou shalt be condemned (Matthew 12:34-37).**

You will speak and produce exactly what you have in your heart—either for good or evil. If your mind is filled with carnality, the only way you will become free is to change what you think.

Control your thoughts by bringing them into obedience to the Scriptures. Program your mind to the Word of God. If you don't, you will be leaving yourself open to lasciviousness. Once the seed of it is planted, it will mature. Before long, you will be saying and doing things you know you shouldn't. Unrestrained thoughts result in unrestrained actions. So put a stop to them quickly by looking to Jesus.

Did you ever notice how easy it is to control your thoughts when you are in a Believers' Convention or in church? That's because in a spiritual atmosphere of the Word and praise and worship, your spirit becomes the dominating force. If you will gauge your whole life around spiritual activities, your inner man can be in control all of the time. Galatians 5:16 says that if you walk in the spirit, you will not fulfill the lusts of the flesh. You see, you can't do two things at once. If you're walking in the spirit, your flesh has to come in line.

You will change what you think as you look to Jesus, the Author and Finisher of your faith. Keep your mind and heart fixed on the Word— on Jesus. He is the only One Who can help you overcome. The Word is spirit and it is life. When your mind is totally saturated with the Word of God, your spirit will exercise its authority to overcome every ungodly thought and evil habit.

A few years ago someone said to me, "Boy, Brother Copeland, you sure have lost a lot of weight!" I said, "No, I didn't. I stopped lasciviousness from operating in my life, and the weight took care of itself." I took my attention off myself and got it on Jesus.

Your victory will come in the same way. As you live in harmony with Jesus, you'll turn your back on the lusts of the flesh. So, if sin has got you in a stronghold, break loose by getting your mind off yourself and looking to Jesus! You can't do two things at the same time. If you turn toward Him, you'll leave that sin behind you!

But you must be determined to fulfill God's Word at any price. Don't compromise. Boldly believe and act on the Word, and your flesh will submit to the control of the Holy Spirit.

Don't let Satan deceive you into sacrificing the glory of God in your life for a few moments of self-indulgence and sin. Restrain your thought life! Meditate the Word instead of selfish, carnal thoughts! Keep your eyes on Jesus, the Author and Finisher of your faith. He's given you the power to be forever free!

# Prayer for Salvation and Baptism in the Holy Spirit

Heavenly Father, I come to You in the Name of Jesus. Your Word says, *"Whosoever shall call on the name of the Lord shall be saved"* (Acts 2:21). I am calling on You. I pray and ask Jesus to come into my heart and be Lord over my life, according to Romans 10:9-10: *"If thou shalt confess with thy mouth the Lord Jesus, and shalt believe in thine heart that God hath raised him from the dead, thou shalt be saved. For with the heart man believeth unto righteousness; and with the mouth confession is made unto salvation."* I do that now. I confess that Jesus is Lord, and I believe in my heart that God raised Him from the dead.

I am now reborn! I am a Christian—a child of Almighty God! I am saved! You also said in Your Word, *"If ye then, being evil, know how to give good gifts unto your children: HOW MUCH MORE shall your heavenly Father give the Holy Spirit to them that ask him?"* (Luke 11:13). I'm also asking You to fill me with the Holy Spirit. Holy Spirit, rise up within me as I praise God. I fully expect to speak with other tongues as You give me utterance (Acts 2:4).

Begin to praise God for filling you with the Holy Spirit. Speak those words and syllables you receive—not in your own language, but the language given to you by the Holy Spirit. You have to use your own voice. God will not force you to speak. Worship and praise Him in your heavenly language—in other tongues.

Continue with the blessing God has given you and pray in tongues each day.

You are a born-again, Spirit-filled believer. You'll never be the same!

Find a good Word of God preaching church, and become a part of a church family who will love and care for you as you love and care for them.

We need to be hooked up to each other. It increases our strength in God. It's God's plan for us.

## About the Author

For more than 32 years, Kenneth Copeland has led countless believers on a journey to maturity in the principles of faith, love, healing, prosperity, redemption and righteousness. Through the *Believers Voice of Victory* broadcast—one of the top five Neilsen-rated inspirational programs—and *BVOV Magazine,* he has brought revelation knowledge on the truths of God's Word. He has taught Christians everywhere that they can conquer the problems and challenges life brings through faith in God's Word.

# Books Available from
# Kenneth Copeland Ministries

**by Kenneth Copeland**
* A Ceremony of Marriage
  A Matter of Choice
  Covenant of Blood
  Faith and Patience—The Power Twins
* Freedom From Fear
  Giving and Receiving
  Honor—Walking in Honesty, Truth and Integrity
  How to Conquer Strife
  How to Discipline Your Flesh
  How to Receive Communion
  Living at the End of Time—A Time of Supernatural Increase
  Love Never Fails
  Managing God's Mutual Funds
* Now Are We in Christ Jesus
* Our Covenant With God
* Prayer—Your Foundation for Success
  Prosperity: The Choice Is Yours
  Rumors of War
* Sensitivity of Heart
  Six Steps to Excellence in Ministry
  Sorrow Not! Winning Over Grief and Sorrow
* The Decision Is Yours
* The Force of Faith
* The Force of Righteousness
  The Image of God in You
  The Laws of Prosperity
* The Mercy of God
  The Miraculous Realm of God's Love
  The Outpouring of the Spirit—The Result of Prayer
* The Power of the Tongue
  The Power to Be Forever Free
  The Troublemaker
* The Winning Attitude
  Turn Your Hurts Into Harvests
* Welcome to the Family
* You Are Healed!
  Your Right-Standing With God

**by Gloria Copeland**
* And Jesus Healed Them All
  Are You Ready?
  Build Your Financial Foundation
  Build Yourself an Ark
  Fight On!
  God's Prescription for Divine Health
  God's Success Formula
  God's Will for You
  God's Will for Your Healing
  God's Will is Prosperity
* God's Will Is the Holy Spirit
* Harvest of Health
  Hidden Treasures
  Living Contact
* Love—The Secret to Your Success

No Deposit—No Return
Pleasing the Father
Pressing In—It's Worth It All
Shine On!
The Power to Live a New Life
The Unbeatable Spirit of Faith
* Walk in the Spirit
Walk With God
Well Worth the Wait

## Books Co-Authored by Kenneth and Gloria Copeland
Family Promises
Healing Promises
Prosperity Promises
Protection Promises

From Faith to Faith—A Daily Guide to Victory
From Faith to Faith—A Perpetual Calendar

One Word From God Series
- One Word from God Can Change Your Destiny
- One Word from God Can Change Your Family
- One Word from God Can Change Your Finances
- One Word from God Can Change Your Formula for Success
- One Word from God Can Change Your Health
- One Word from God Can Change Your Nation
- One Word from God Can Change Your Prayer Life
- One Word from God Can Change Your Relationships

Over the Edge—A Youth Devotional
Over the Edge Xtreme Planner for Students—
  Designed for the School Year

Pursuit of His Presence—A Daily Devotional
Pursuit of His Presence—A Perpetual Calendar

## Other Books Published by KCP
The First 30 Years—A Journey of Faith
  The story of the lives of Kenneth and Gloria Copeland
Real People. Real Needs. Real Victories.
  A book of testimonies to encourage your faith.

John G. Lake—His Life, His Sermons, His Boldness of Faith
The Holiest of All, by Andrew Murray
The New Testament in Modern Speech,
  by Richard Francis Weymouth

## Products Designed for Today's Children and Youth
Baby Praise Board Book
Baby Praise Christmas Board Book
Noah's Ark Coloring Book
Shout! Super-Activity Book

## Commander Kellie and the Superkids Adventure Novels
#1     Escape from Jungle Island
#2     In Pursuit of the Enemy
#3     Mysterious Presence, The
#4     Quest for the Second Half, The

SWORD Adventure Book

*Available in Spanish

# World Offices of Kenneth Copeland Ministries

For more information and a free catalog, please write
the office nearest you.

Kenneth Copeland Ministries
Fort Worth, Texas 76192-0001

Kenneth Copeland
Locked Bag 2600
Mansfield Delivery Centre
QUEENSLAND 4122
AUSTRALIA

Kenneth Copeland
Post Office Box 15
BATH
BA1 1GD
ENGLAND U.K.

Kenneth Copeland
Private Bag X 909
FONTAINEBLEAU 2032
REPUBLIC OF SOUTH AFRICA

Kenneth Copeland
Post Office Box 378
SURREY, BC V3T 5B6
CANADA

UKRAINE
L'VIV 290000
Post Office Box 84
Kenneth Copeland
L'VIV 290000
UKRAINE

## The Harrison House Vision

Proclaiming the truth and the power
Of the Gospel of Jesus Christ
With excellence;

Challenging Christians to
Live victoriously,
Grow spiritually,
Know God intimately.